JUL   2013

SECRETS OF Magic

VANISHING TRICKS

STEPHANIE TURNBULL

A⁺
Smart Apple Media

Published by Smart Apple Media
P.O. Box 3263
Mankato, MN 56002

Printed in the United States of America at Corporate Graphics, in North Mankato, Minnesota.

Library of Congress Cataloging-in-Publication Data
Turnbull, Stephanie.
Vanishing tricks / by Stephanie Turnbull.
    p. cm. -- (Secrets of magic)
Includes index.
Summary: "Teaches how to make everyday objects vanish and reappear using techniques
like the paddle move and palming. Includes step-by-step instructions, picture diagrams,
and performance tips"--Provided by publisher.
ISBN 978-1-59920-500-7 (library binding)
1. Magic tricks--Juvenile literature. I. Title.
GV1548.T7 2012
793.8--dc22
                                                          2011000337

Created by Appleseed Editions Ltd.
Designed and illustrated by Guy Callaby
Edited by Mary-Jane Wilkins
Picture research by Su Alexander

Picture credits
l = left, r = right, t = top, b = bottom
Contents page l Eline Spek/Shutterstock, r Ljupco Smokovski/Shutterstock; 4t William Callis/Shutterstock, b
upthebanner/Shutterstock; 5l Reuters/Corbis, r Kruchankova Maya/Shutterstock; 7 Photos 12/Alamy; 8 Tom
Baker/Shutterstock; 9t Zdorovkirill Vladimirovich/Shutterstock, Tischenko Irina/Shutterstock, cl Margo
Harrison/Shutterstock, r Eric Isselee/Shutterstock, b Ljupco Smokovski/Shutterstock; 12 Lia Koltyrina/
Shutterstock; 16 Tiorna/Shutterstock; 17 Borislav Toskov/Shutterstock; 18 Zaneta Baranowska/Shutterstock;
19 The Protected Art Archive/Alamy; 20 Ivonne Wierink/Shutterstock; 21 Elena Schweitzer/Shutterstock;
24l Brett Stoltz/Shutterstock, r C./Shutterstock; 26 Peter Kim/Shutterstock; 27 Corbis; 28 Lisa F Young/
Shutterstock
Front Cover: Lia Koltyrina/Shutterstock

DAD0049E
6-2012

9 8 7 6 5 4 3

Contents

Now You See It...

In some magic shows, the magician dramatically appears or disappears in a big puff of smoke, which conveniently hides any sneaky moves!

IF YOU WANT to become a magician, you'll need a few great vanishing tricks to amaze your friends. The tricks in this book are perfect as they all use small, everyday **props** such as coins, bandannas, matchboxes, and paperclips, so they're not expensive —and many are simpler than you might think!

LARGE-SCALE VANISHES

Some magicians specialize in elaborate **illusions** on stage or TV, in which they make people, large objects, or even whole buildings disappear—the bigger, the better! Many of these effects use mirrors, trapdoors, or complicated equipment with hidden wires. In one of the biggest illusions ever, the magician David Copperfield made the Statue of Liberty disappear. Can you think how? Go to page 32 to read one theory.

The Statue of Liberty is 305 feet (93 m) tall and has a whole museum in its enormous base. How did David Copperfield make it vanish?

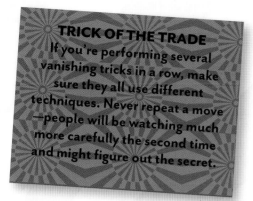
MASTER MAGICIAN

P.C. SORCAR, JR.

(born 1946)

The illusionist P.C. Sorcar, Jr. is the son of famous Indian magician P.C. Sorcar, Sr. As a boy, Sorcar Jr. helped his father on stage and then began performing on his own. He is known for lavish shows that include laser light displays and many singing and dancing assistants. His spectacular tricks include making an aircraft, a museum, and a train (complete with passengers) disappear. His biggest stunt was making the famous Taj Mahal in Agra, India, vanish for a full two minutes.

CLEVER CLOSE-UP MOVES

The disadvantage of big stage illusions is that the audience has to view them from a distance at a certain angle, or they'll spot the trick. Many magicians prefer smaller, close-up tricks that use clever **sleight-of-hand** moves, such as **palming** a coin so neatly that people standing next to them have no idea where it's gone.

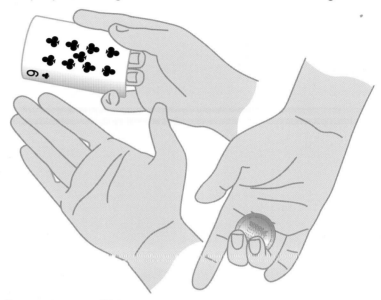

PRODUCTION TRICKS

If you make something disappear, then usually you want to make it reappear too—sometimes from a different place. Tricks in which things appear are often called productions. Production tricks can be just as spectacular as vanishing tricks!

One famous production trick is to pull a rabbit out of a hat. Find out who invented it on page 10.

Tricks of the Trade

TRICK OF THE TRADE
In many vanishing tricks, you pretend to perform certain actions, such as picking up a coin. Film yourself picking it up and then copy those actions for the fake move. This will help make your sleights more realistic.

THE KEY TO being a great magician is to remember three Ps: practice, **patter**, and performance. Practice comes first. You need to practice each trick until you get the moves just right. Once you've mastered a few tricks, think about your patter and performance style. Never be tempted to show a trick before you're ready!

PERFECT PATTER

Patter is what you say as you perform. It lets you introduce tricks and keeps your audience entertained. Patter is also a very important way of distracting people while you move or hide something you don't want them to notice. This technique is called **misdirection** and is something every magician uses. For example, if you tell people to look at something, then they will—as long as you do too!

SMOOTH MOVES

Be confident when you perform. Make your moves bold and graceful. This will make you appear more professional and your tricks look more effective. It's a good idea to practice in front of a mirror, so you can check that you're holding props correctly—or, even better, film yourself. You can find extra performance tips on pages 28 and 29.

OK, I'll hold the coin tightly in my fist . . .

The coin is really in this hand.

THE SURPRISE VANISH
This trick is a perfect example of misdirection.

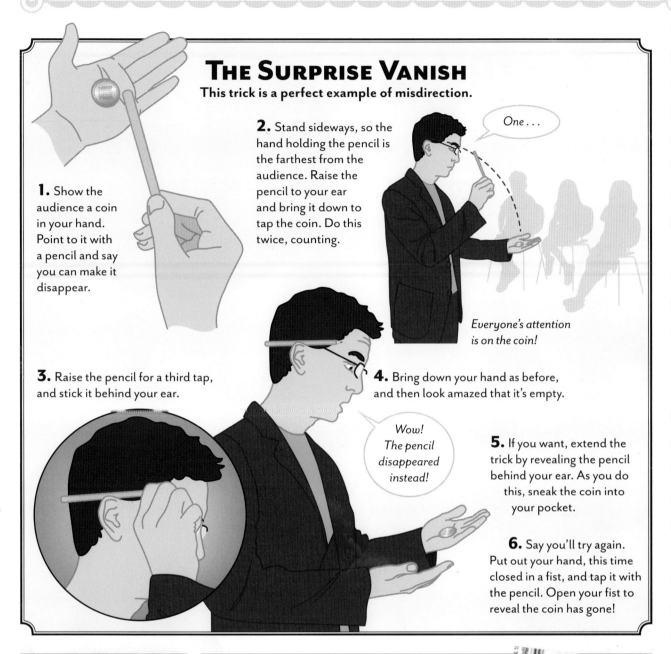

1. Show the audience a coin in your hand. Point to it with a pencil and say you can make it disappear.

2. Stand sideways, so the hand holding the pencil is the farthest from the audience. Raise the pencil to your ear and bring it down to tap the coin. Do this twice, counting.

One . . .

Everyone's attention is on the coin!

3. Raise the pencil for a third tap, and stick it behind your ear.

4. Bring down your hand as before, and then look amazed that it's empty.

Wow! The pencil disappeared instead!

5. If you want, extend the trick by revealing the pencil behind your ear. As you do this, sneak the coin into your pocket.

6. Say you'll try again. Put out your hand, this time closed in a fist, and tap it with the pencil. Open your fist to reveal the coin has gone!

MASTER MAGICIAN

CHANNING POLLOCK (1926–2006)

Channing Pollock was an American magician famous for his sophisticated, elegant stage act. He was always smartly dressed and performed tricks with graceful **flourishes** that kept audiences enthralled. He is best known for making doves appear from his hands, as if he were shaping them out of thin air. He created his calm, cool persona to mask the fact that he was really very nervous on stage. He was so good at acting that he later retired from magic to become a film actor instead.

Silly Stuff

IF YOU WANT to grab people's attention, you need a few funny vanishing tricks to make everyone laugh—and to keep them wanting more. Here are some great ideas to try out on your friends at a party!

DISAPPEARING CUPCAKE

Here's a vanishing riddle to start with. Put a cupcake on the table. Say you'll leave the room and the cake will have vanished before you walk back in—even though nobody else will touch it. Can you guess how? Turn to page 32 for the answer!

WHERE'S MY LEG?

You won't fool people with this gag, but it looks great!

Well, it's a start!

audience view

reverse view

Practice balancing on one leg without wobbling!

1. Hold a long towel or coat in front of you, so just the tips of your shoes are showing. Make sure your shoes are loose, so you can slip out of them easily.

2. Tell people you are trying to learn how to vanish, but you haven't quite mastered it. As you talk, slip one foot out of your shoe and bend your leg up behind you.

3. Slowly lift up the towel to reveal that one of your legs has gone.

EAR AND NOSE CANDY VANISH

This trick is gross but very funny if you do it convincingly.

1. Hold out three small candies, such as Tic Tacs, in your left hand. Say, "Did you know that all the cavities in my head link to my mouth? I'll show you."

2. Say, "I take one candy at a time and lubricate it a little . . ." Cup your left hand around the candies and reach over with your right hand to take one. In fact, you pick up TWO candies.

3. Put the candies in your mouth. Tuck one away in your cheek and swish the other around in your mouth. While you do this, make your left hand into a fist.

4. Take out the candy and place it on top of your fist. Use your right hand to push your hair behind your right ear. Say, "Now I put the candy in my ear."

5. Pretend to pick up the candy again, but brush it into your left fist.

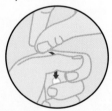

6. Pretend to lift the candy to your ear and carefully push it right inside.

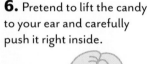

7. Open your fist to show that two candies are still there, and pick up the second. As in step 2, pick up two candies. Say, "This one needs to go up my nose. Let me wet it first."

8. Put the candies in your mouth as in step 3 and again tuck one into your cheek. Take one candy out and place it on your fist, as in step 4, while you rub your nose and sniff a few times.

9. Brush the candy into your fist again, as in step 5, and pretend to snort it up your nose.

10. Open your fist to show the last candy. Say, "And the last one goes in my mouth." Pop it in.

11. Now tilt your head back and forth and massage your ears and nose. Say, "I can move the candies through my cavities . . . so they reappear in my mouth!" One by one, spit the three candies on to your hand!

Tell people not to copy you—it's dangerous to push objects into your ears or nose!

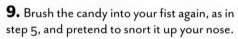

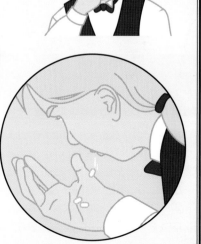

Animal Magic

OVER THE YEARS, magicians have baffled audiences by making animals disappear or by producing them from unusual or impossibly small places. Here are a few famous animal tricks, plus one you can do yourself—without harming any real animals!

THE BIRDCAGE VANISH

A French magician called Buatier de Kolta created a famous effect using a bird. He held up a wire cage with the bird inside and then made a sudden movement—and the cage and bird were gone. In modern versions, the bird is usually a fake one.

DONKEYS AND ELEPHANTS

Small birds weren't much use to stage magicians—they needed big animals that everyone could see! One illusionist called Charles Morritt invented a trick with a donkey. He led the donkey into a large box on wheels and closed the doors. He then reopened them to show the box was empty. He sold his idea to the famous magician Harry Houdini, who went one step farther and used an elephant instead.

Houdini's elephant trick was a big success and he performed it many times. Have you guessed how it was done? Turn to page 32 to find out.

MASTER MAGICIAN

JOHN HENRY ANDERSON (1814–1874)

You may not have heard of the Scottish conjurer John Henry Anderson, but you do know his most famous trick—pulling a white rabbit out of a top hat. This trick usually uses some sort of gimmick (see pages 26–27). Anderson called himself "The Great Wizard of the North" and performed many other brilliant effects, including a bottle that magically produced any drink requested by members of the audience! He toured the world and even performed for Queen Victoria.

THE MAGICAL (PAPER) RABBIT

1. Find a large, empty matchbox and a piece of card stock or thick paper that fits inside the tray.

2. Draw a rabbit on the card.

3. Cut the matchbox tray in two, about two-thirds of the way along.

short piece

long piece

4. Put the tray pieces back in the sleeve. Put a tiny mark on the long piece so you recognize it. Now you're ready to perform.

5. Tell people that you can make your rabbit disappear. Hold the matchbox with the long end at the top. Push up the bottom end with your finger to open the tray and then slip the rabbit inside.

6. Push the tray down to close it. Push up the short end a tiny bit and then pull up the long end with your other hand. The rabbit stays in the bottom piece of the tray.

Make sure that people aren't close enough to see inside the matchbox.

7. Close the tray again and say you'll make the rabbit come back. This time, push the bottom half of the tray much farther up so that the rabbit is pushed up too. Hey presto—he's back!

TRICK OF THE TRADE
Practice both ways of pushing up the tray so your fingers are in an almost identical position each time. This makes it harder for people to spot the secret!

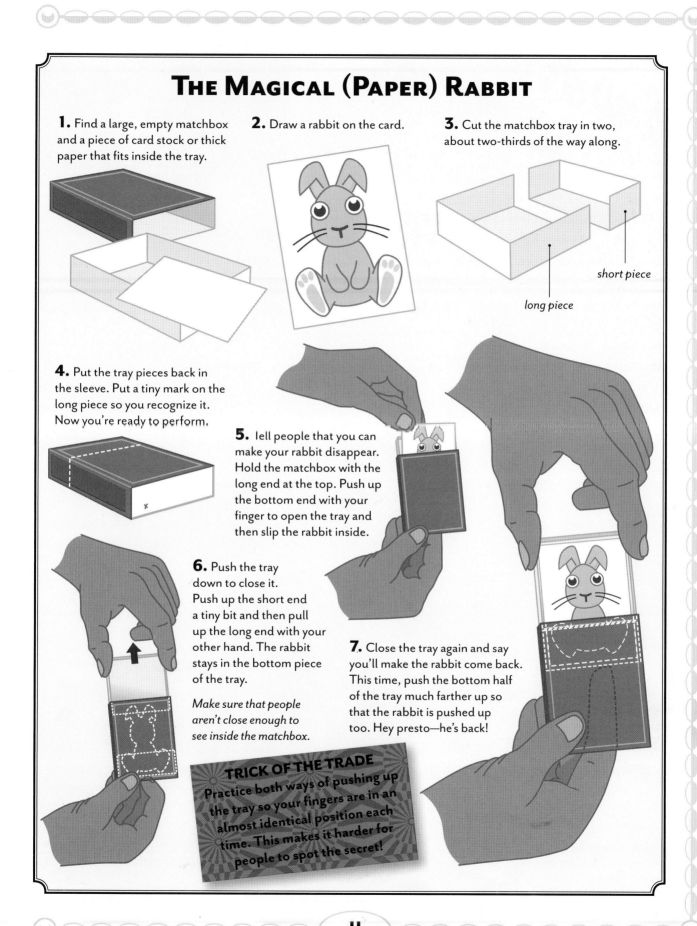

Handy Hand Moves

IF YOU'VE TRIED the Ear and Nose Candy Vanish on page 9, then congratulations—you now know a sleight-of-hand move. Sleights are very useful, as you can make things "disappear" just by moving them to your other hand or dropping them out of sight.

THE FRENCH DROP

One well-known sleight is called the French Drop. Here's how you do it with a coin.

1. Hold a coin in your right hand between your thumb and index finger.

2. Put your left hand over the coin, as if you're about to take it, but then drop it into your right hand.

3. Close your left hand in a fist, as if the coin is inside, and move it away. Leave your right hand loosely cupped with the coin hidden inside.

4. Hold out your left fist and make sure everyone's attention is on it. Shake it or blow on it. Then dramatically uncurl your fingers to reveal that the coin has vanished.

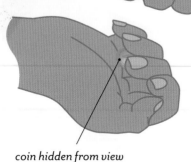

coin hidden from view

Drop the coin on to your lap or sneak it into your pocket while everyone is distracted by your empty left hand.

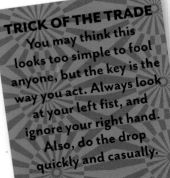

TRICK OF THE TRADE
You may think this looks too simple to fool anyone, but the key is the way you act. Always look at your left fist, and ignore your right hand. Also, do the drop quickly and casually.

MEIR YEDID

Israeli-born magician Meir Yedid is a sleight-of-hand expert who can make all kinds of things vanish from his hands. In fact, he doesn't even need props—he can make his own fingers seem to disappear. The strange thing is that one of the fingers on his right hand really is missing (as a result of a car accident), but this doesn't mean he cheats—he performs all the tricks using his left hand, while hiding the fact that one of his right fingers isn't there!

THE HUMAN PIGGY-BANK

**Here's a good way of using the French Drop in a trick.
Use your imagination to think of some more!**

1. Hold up a coin in your right hand. Say, "Did you know I store my spare cash in my arms? Really! Let me show you."

Hang on . . . it's here somewhere . . .

2. Point to your left elbow and explain that you have a hidden slot to put coins in. With your left arm bent and your left hand resting against your neck, rub the coin around on your elbow, as if trying to find the slot.

3. Pretend to be confused. Say, "Oh, wait . . . it must be in the other elbow! Sorry . . ." As you talk, hold up your right elbow, and appear to move the coin to your left hand so you can post it in the slot. In fact, French Drop it so it stays in your right hand.

4. Put your right arm in the same position as your left arm in step 2 and sneakily drop the coin down the back of your neck. Meanwhile, rub your left hand on your elbow as if you're searching for the spot again.

5. With a satisfied, "Ah, got it!" slap your left hand on your elbow and take it away to show that the coin has disappeared into the magical slot.

Focus on your elbow—not on your hands.

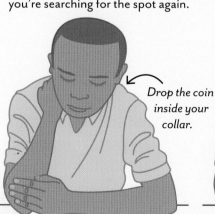

Drop the coin inside your collar.

Make sure your shirt is tucked in so the coin doesn't fall out!

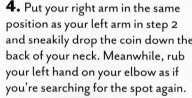

Perfect Palming

ONCE YOU'VE MASTERED the French Drop, you may want to try some sleights called palms. A palm is a clever way of holding a small object so that your hand looks empty. Palms are difficult, but when you get them right, they look great!

Many magicians do amazing palms with cards, but you may find it easiest to stick with coins. Cards are hard to hide if you have small hands!

Finger Palm

This is probably the easiest palm to learn. Take a coin and bend your two middle fingers to hold it in place. Let the other fingers curl a little, too. From the audience's side, your hand looks empty. Hold it naturally and misdirect the audience's attention by doing something interesting with your other hand.

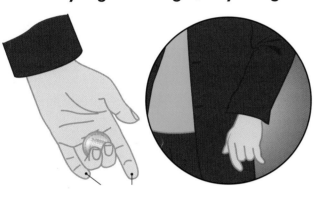

Classic Palm

This is a neat palm, but it's tricky to do. Press a coin into your palm and hold it in place by squeezing the fleshy base of your thumb over it. Then straighten your fingers as much as you can.

TRICK OF THE TRADE
Be patient—palms take time to perfect. Keep a coin in your pocket so you can practice during spare time.

EDGE PALM

An edge palm is a great way of making a coin disappear and appear again. Some magicians can edge palm more than ten coins in one hand!

1. Hold a coin between your fingers, like this.

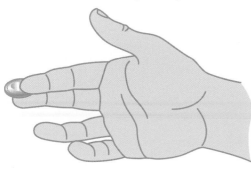

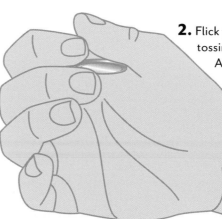

2. Flick your hand as if you're tossing the coin into the air. As you do this, curl your fingers around and wedge the coin between your thumb and index finger.

3. Straighten your fingers. From the front or back, your hand looks empty.

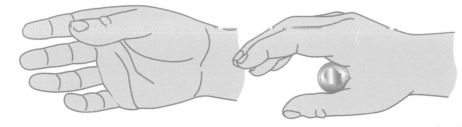

audience view   *view from above*

4. Now flick your hand as before and curl your fingers again to grab the coin. If you do it fast enough, it looks as though you plucked the coin out of thin air.

USING PALMS IN TRICKS

Once you've learned a palming method, you can make a coin magically appear from anywhere you want. For example, you could hold a bag or cup (using your hand with the palmed coin in it), show that it's empty, and then drop the coin in it as if it fell from the sky.

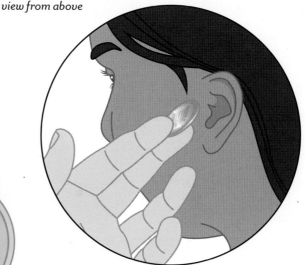

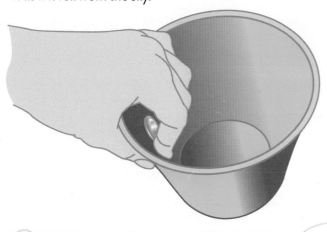

Another idea is to pretend to pluck the coin from a friend's ear, hair, or clothes.

You could even hold your nose with your hand and let the coin fall, as if you squeezed it out of a nostril!

Crafty Hiding Places

MANY VANISHING TRICKS involve hiding objects somewhere on yourself—for example, up your sleeve or in your pocket. The great thing about these tricks is that, unlike palms, the object really has gone from your hands, so there's no chance of accidentally dropping it!

TOP POCKET VANISH

For this trick, you need a shirt or jacket with a top pocket.

1. Hold a coin in your left hand and a bandanna or scarf in your right hand.

hold bandanna by one corner

2. Hold up your left hand so it's in line with your top pocket. Drape the bandanna over the coin and drag it toward you, keeping your left hand still.

coin is under bandanna

pocket

3. Keep going until the bandanna comes off to reveal the coin, still in your left hand. By now, your right hand should be touching your jacket front.

4. Put the bandanna over your left hand again, as if you're going to repeat step 2. But this time, secretly grip the coin under your right thumb.

5. Keep dragging the bandanna toward you, as in step 2, as if the coin is still in your left hand. When your right hand reaches your jacket front, drop the coin into the pocket.

coin drops into pocket

6. As the bandanna comes off your left hand, everyone can see that the coin has gone. Show both hands and shake out the bandanna to prove it really has disappeared!

CRISS ANGEL

(born 1967)

*The brilliantly simple toothpick idea on this page belongs to the Greek-American illusionist and **escapologist** Criss Angel. Although Angel often performs large-scale, extreme illusions such as floating above a tall building, walking on water, or apparently cutting himself in half, he is also an expert in small sleight-of-hand techniques. He uses these as part of **street magic** routines, where he stops people outdoors and stuns them with one or two quick effects.*

TRICK OF THE TRADE

Think about your costume when planning vanishing or production tricks. Long sleeves, pockets, stiff collars, or hoods could all be useful places to hide objects such as coins. Always wear the outfit when you practice so you know exactly which hiding places work.

QUICK TOOTHPICK TRICK
A simple, effective vanishing trick

1. Before you perform, tape a toothpick on to your thumbnail with a small piece of clear tape.

2. Slide out the stick so you're left with a raised loop of tape.

3. Show the audience the toothpick and your empty hands.

They don't see the tiny piece of tape.

4. Make a fist with your thumb inside and pretend to grip the toothpick in your fist. In fact, slide the stick into the loop in the tape.

5. Concentrate on the stick and then suddenly open your hand. It's gone!

audience view   *your view*

6. Now pretend to snatch the stick out of the air, quickly making your hand back into a fist. Pull out the stick with your other hand and show people that it really is an ordinary stick!

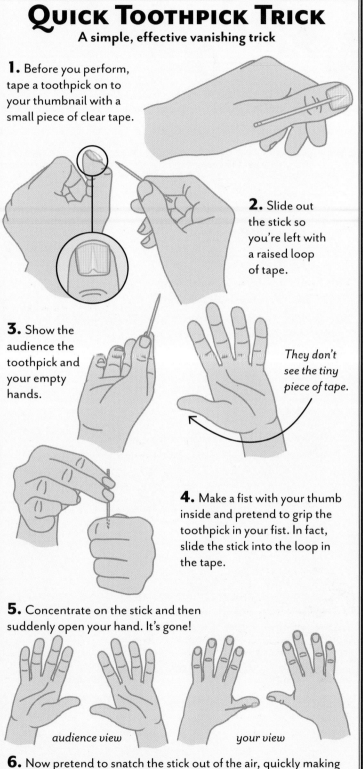

A Knot... or Not?

MAKING A KNOT disappear from a scarf or rope is a famous magical effect. There are lots of different ways to do this, and the good news is that many methods are surprisingly simple. Here are two ideas to try.

FREE THE BANGLES

This knot vanish is a self-working trick—in other words, it doesn't use sleight-of-hand, and as long as you follow the steps exactly, it will work every time.

1. Ask a volunteer to hold out a pencil. Drape two long pieces of string (or shoelaces) over the pencil.

2. Hold one doubled string in each hand and tie a single knot. Pull it tight.

pull tight

3. Now take two metal or plastic bangles and ask your volunteer to thread one on to each end of the doubled strings.

4. Take one strand of each doubled string and tie them in a single knot over the bangles. Make sure it's tight. Hand the strands back to the volunteer so they're holding both doubled strings again.

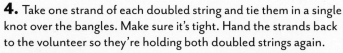

pull tight

5. Say, "So there's no way the bangles can escape, right? They're tied on and you're holding the ends of the string." Now quickly pull out the pencil and the knots will disappear.

Let people examine everything afterward so they know you're not using trick props.

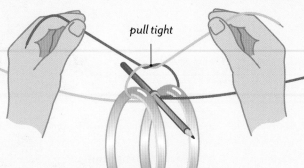

SPEEDY KNOT VANISH

This quick, effective vanish needs a lot of practice.

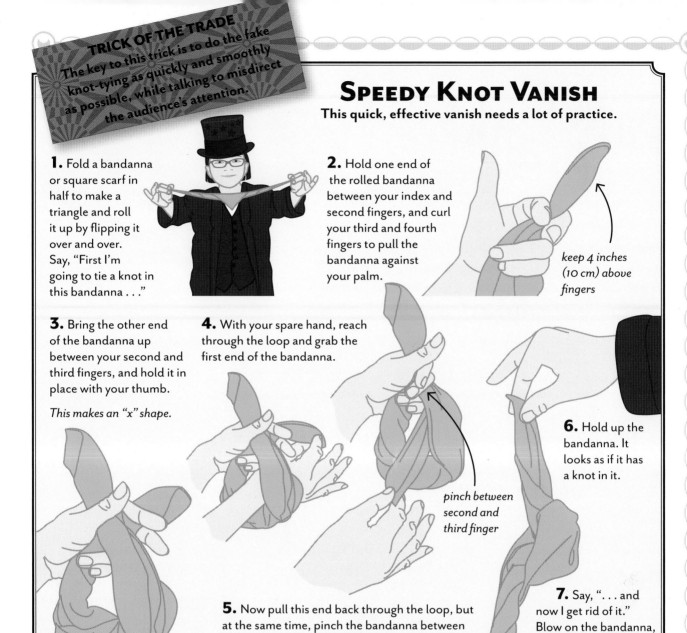

1. Fold a bandanna or square scarf in half to make a triangle and roll it up by flipping it over and over. Say, "First I'm going to tie a knot in this bandanna . . ."

2. Hold one end of the rolled bandanna between your index and second fingers, and curl your third and fourth fingers to pull the bandanna against your palm.

keep 4 inches (10 cm) above fingers

3. Bring the other end of the bandanna up between your second and third fingers, and hold it in place with your thumb.

This makes an "x" shape.

4. With your spare hand, reach through the loop and grab the first end of the bandanna.

pinch between second and third finger

5. Now pull this end back through the loop, but at the same time, pinch the bandanna between your second and third fingers. This traps a bunch of the bandanna in the loop, creating a **slipknot**.

6. Hold up the bandanna. It looks as if it has a knot in it.

7. Say, ". . . and now I get rid of it." Blow on the bandanna, pull both ends, and the knot vanishes.

MASTER MAGICIAN

DANTE (1883–1955)

Dante was born in Denmark but grew up in America. He toured theaters around the world with a large group of performers and also appeared on TV and in films. He was famous for his nonsense phrase, "Sim Sala Bim," which has since been used by other magicians instead of "Abracadabra." Free the Bangles is adapted from one of Dante's well-known tricks. He called it The Lazy Magician because he used to sit back and make his two assistants do all the work for him!

Paper Pranks

VANISHING TRICKS ARE more impressive when done with everyday items rather than fancy magic shop supplies. Try these tricks using ordinary pieces of paper, and then test them out on your friends in the classroom.

THE TORN-UP COIN
Borrow a quarter or dime from a friend for this trick.

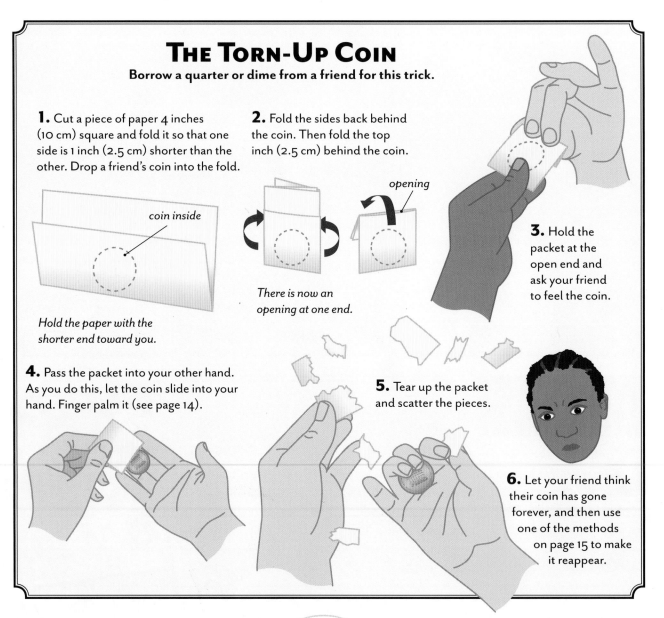

1. Cut a piece of paper 4 inches (10 cm) square and fold it so that one side is 1 inch (2.5 cm) shorter than the other. Drop a friend's coin into the fold.

coin inside

Hold the paper with the shorter end toward you.

2. Fold the sides back behind the coin. Then fold the top inch (2.5 cm) behind the coin.

opening

There is now an opening at one end.

3. Hold the packet at the open end and ask your friend to feel the coin.

4. Pass the packet into your other hand. As you do this, let the coin slide into your hand. Finger palm it (see page 14).

5. Tear up the packet and scatter the pieces.

6. Let your friend think their coin has gone forever, and then use one of the methods on page 15 to make it reappear.

ROBERT HARBIN (1909–1978)

Robert Harbin was born in South Africa but moved to London as a young man. He became a well-known TV magician as well as an inventor of props for big stage illusions and a writer of books on magic. He performed clever effects with paper, such as tearing up a newspaper, stacking the pieces, and then unfolding them to reveal that the newspaper was whole again. He also became fascinated with origami, the Japanese art of paper-folding, and wrote many books on the subject.

PAPER FOLD VANISH
This trick involves some sneaky preparation beforehand.

1. Cut two identical pieces of thick paper, about 3.5 inches (9 cm) square. Fold each piece into thirds both ways, making nine equal squares.

2. Fold each piece of paper into a packet, with the middle square as the back. Stick them together, back to back.

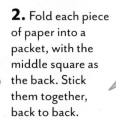

glue here

3. Unfold one piece and keep the other folded and hidden behind so it looks as if there's only one piece of paper.

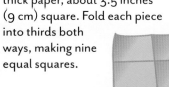

folded packet stuck behind

4. Now you're ready to perform. Put a coin in the center of the paper. Fold the paper around it.

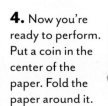

5. Hold up the pack and announce that you'll make the coin disappear. Bring it down again and, as you do, casually turn it over. Now the empty piece of paper is on top.

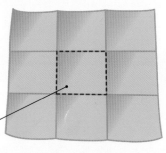

6. Slowly unfold the paper to show that the coin has disappeared.

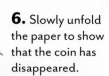

TRICK OF THE TRADE
Don't use thin paper for this trick, as the second folded piece will be visible under the top piece. Experiment until you find paper that works well.

7. Reverse the process to make the coin reappear.

The Paddle Move

ANOTHER CLEVER WAY of making something seem to appear or disappear is a sleight called the paddle move. You turn an object in your hand and give it an extra secret twist, so you rotate it more than the audience realizes. The best way to understand how it works is to give it a try!

LEARNING THE MOVE

You can buy paddles from magic shops, but a butter knife works just as well. First, stick something on one side, such as a sticker or a moistened bit of paper. Hold the knife so that it rests on your fingers with your thumb on top.

sticker

Say that you have stickers on both sides of the knife. To "prove" this, move the knife so it's upright in your hand, but at the same time, use your thumb and index finger to twist the knife around. You seem to be showing the other side of the knife, but you're actually showing the same side.

The bigger motion of moving your hand up hides the smaller motion of twisting the knife.

Do this a few times to make it clear that there are stickers on both sides. Now say you can make them disappear. Blow on the knife and, at the same time, quickly move your hand up without the extra twist. Now you're showing the side of the knife with no sticker.

Use the paddle move again to show that the sticker has disappeared from the other side of the knife, too. Of course you're showing the same side each time, keeping the sticker side hidden.

TRICK OF THE TRADE
You need to do the paddle move quickly for it to work properly. Once you've got the hang of it, you can make the stickers appear and disappear again and again.

THE MONEY-MAKING MACHINE

This production trick uses exactly the same paddle move but has a few extra props to make it look more impressive.

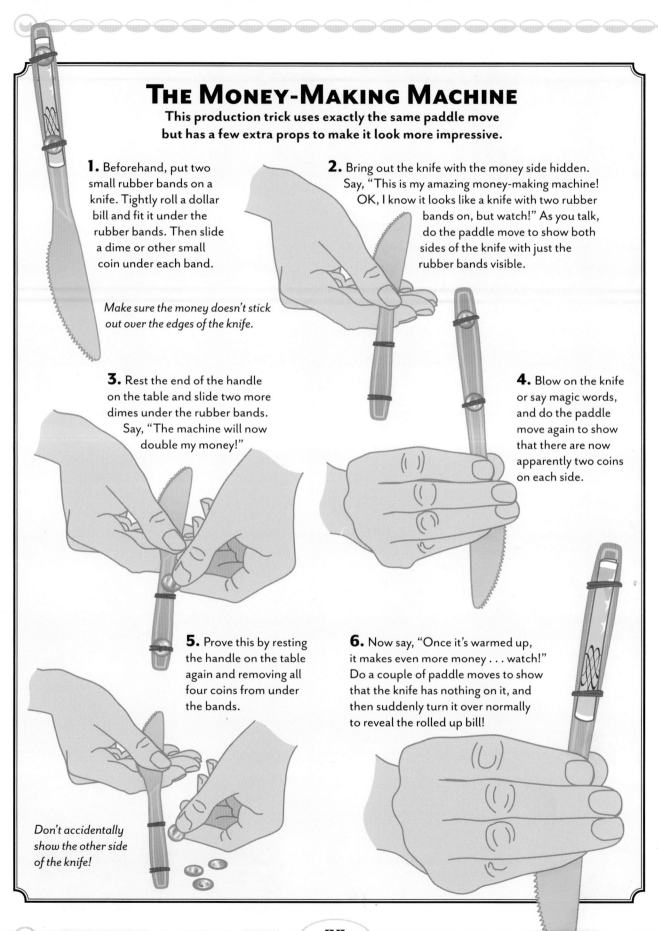

1. Beforehand, put two small rubber bands on a knife. Tightly roll a dollar bill and fit it under the rubber bands. Then slide a dime or other small coin under each band.

Make sure the money doesn't stick out over the edges of the knife.

2. Bring out the knife with the money side hidden. Say, "This is my amazing money-making machine! OK, I know it looks like a knife with two rubber bands on, but watch!" As you talk, do the paddle move to show both sides of the knife with just the rubber bands visible.

3. Rest the end of the handle on the table and slide two more dimes under the rubber bands. Say, "The machine will now double my money!"

4. Blow on the knife or say magic words, and do the paddle move again to show that there are now apparently two coins on each side.

5. Prove this by resting the handle on the table again and removing all four coins from under the bands.

Don't accidentally show the other side of the knife!

6. Now say, "Once it's warmed up, it makes even more money . . . watch!" Do a couple of paddle moves to show that the knife has nothing on it, and then suddenly turn it over normally to reveal the rolled up bill!

Mealtime Magic

A GOOD PLACE to do magic is at the dinner table, where you have a ready-made audience. You're also surrounded by props—for example, knives for the paddle move (pages 22–23) and napkins for a Speedy Knot Vanish (page 19). If you're in a café with packets of salt, pepper, and sugar, you can try these fun food tricks.

SALTY OR SWEET?

This trick makes a packet of salt vanish and produces a packet of sugar, but you could alter it to suit whatever props are on the table.

1. Before you start, sneakily take a packet of sugar and finger palm it in your left hand.

See page 14 for finger palming.

2. With your right hand, pull out a packet of salt and say, "Have you ever sprinkled sugar on your food instead of salt? It's such an easy mistake to make! See, it's salt . . ." As you talk, casually toss the packet on to the table near the edge.

See, it's salt . . .

3. Now appear to scoop up the packet again with your right hand, but really slide it toward you over the table and let it drop into your lap.

When you practice, first pick up the packet and then copy that move for the sleight.

4. Hold up your hand as if the packet is inside, while saying, ". . . but sometimes, when you look again . . ." Bring your left hand up and rub the two together.

5. Now open your hands and finish, ". . . you find it was sugar all along!"

TRICK OF THE TRADE
If you're not comfortable palming the sugar, just practice step 3 and turn this into a simple vanishing trick.

THE EVAPORATING SUGAR

1. Before you perform, sneak a packet of sugar out of the bowl. Under the table, pinch the sides of the packet and make a small tear across one side near the top. Shake out the sugar.

small tear

2. Secretly replace the empty sugar packet in the bowl.

3. Say, "Did you know sugar **evaporates** in your hand?" Reach for the bowl and take your packet. Tear off the top, along the tear you ripped earlier.

Now nobody will know there was already a tear in the packet.

4. Open the top of the packet and pretend to pour the sugar into your fist.

5. Shake out any grains at the bottom of the packet so it looks more realistic. Then crumple it up and throw it on the table.

6. Hold up your fist and say, "As your hand heats the sugar, it melts and eventually . . ."—open your fingers—". . . disappears!"

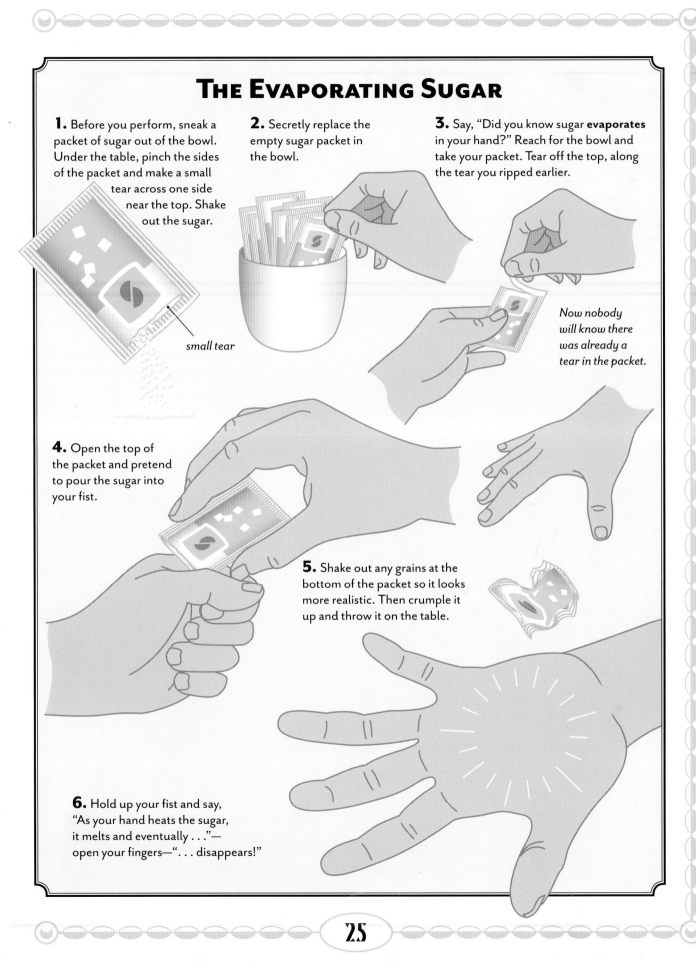

Great Gimmicks

SOME VANISHING TRICKS use props called gimmicks with false bottoms, hidden compartments, or other secret features. You can buy these from magic shops, but beware—good equipment is expensive and may only be useful for one trick. Why not save your money and try this homemade gimmick instead?

Some magicians use gimmicks such as fake flowers that spring out of a wand or tiny box when a switch is pressed.

MAKING A PULL

Here's how to make a piece of magical equipment called a **pull**. Follow these steps, and then use your pull in the trick opposite.

1. Link two rubber bands together. To do this, lie two bands together, like this.

Pull one end of the second band up through the first . . .

. . . then feed that end back under the second band . . .

. . . and pull it tight to make a knot.

2. Add another band in the same way. Now thread a paperclip on to one end.

3. Put one band around your arm just below the elbow. You should be able to hold the paperclip in your hand with the other bands stretched tight. If it's not long enough, add another rubber band. If it's too long, move it farther up your arm.

Make sure the rubber band around your arm isn't so tight it's uncomfortable.

WHERE DID THAT PAPERCLIP GO?

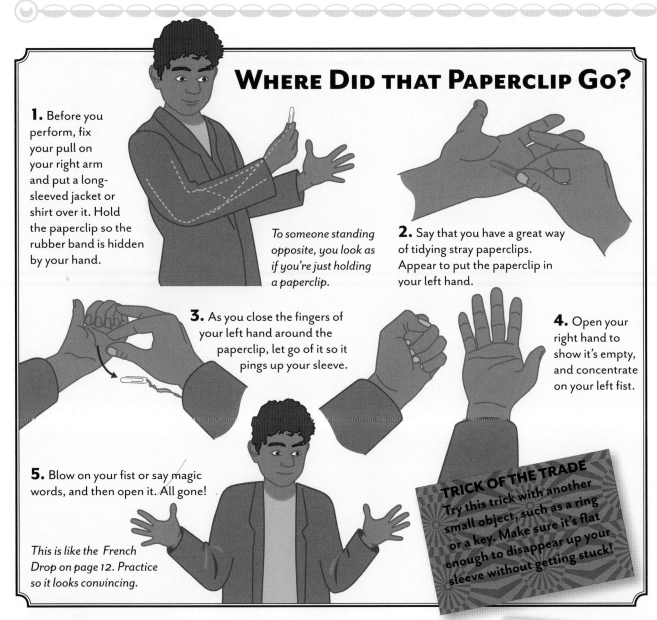

1. Before you perform, fix your pull on your right arm and put a long-sleeved jacket or shirt over it. Hold the paperclip so the rubber band is hidden by your hand.

To someone standing opposite, you look as if you're just holding a paperclip.

2. Say that you have a great way of tidying stray paperclips. Appear to put the paperclip in your left hand.

3. As you close the fingers of your left hand around the paperclip, let go of it so it pings up your sleeve.

4. Open your right hand to show it's empty, and concentrate on your left fist.

5. Blow on your fist or say magic words, and then open it. All gone!

This is like the French Drop on page 12. Practice so it looks convincing.

TRICK OF THE TRADE
Try this trick with another small object, such as a ring or a key. Make sure it's flat enough to disappear up your sleeve without getting stuck!

MASTER MAGICIAN

HARRY KELLAR (1849–1922)

The American magician Harry Kellar performed many impressive vanishes using complicated gimmicks full of hidden mechanisms and wires. In one of his routines, he covered a lit lamp with a cloth and shot at it with a pistol. The lamp melted away and the cloth fell to the ground. Once, the mechanism didn't work, and the lamp stayed where it was. Kellar had to design a new, more reliable prop! A rival, Alexander Herrmann (see page 29), criticized Kellar for using gimmicks instead of doing sleights, but Kellar argued that his tricks were just as clever because they all required great misdirection skills to work well.

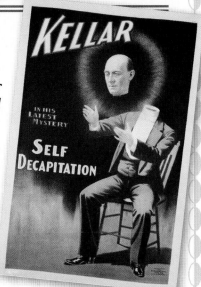

KELLAR

IN HIS LATEST MYSTERY

SELF DECAPITATION

Show Time!

ONCE YOU'VE LEARNED some vanishing tricks and practiced until they're perfect, you may want to put on a magic show for your friends or family. Here are some hints and tips which will make your performance a success.

PERFECT PLANNING

Make sure your act has variety—for example, do several types of vanishes with a range of props. Don't overwhelm people by trying to cram in too many tricks. Save a few for another time! Take your time and present each trick confidently and enthusiastically. If you're having fun, the audience will, too.

MAKING AN IMPACT

A great performance isn't just about tricks—the way you look and act is important as well. Many magicians use quirky costumes to capture the audience's attention, perhaps by looking spooky and mysterious or maybe comical and clownish. Find an outfit that you feel comfortable wearing.

If you're not planning to hide props up your sleeves or in your pockets, try wearing simple clothes so everyone can see you have nothing to hide!

ALEXANDER HERRMANN (1844–1896)

The French magician Alexander Herrmann, often known as Herrmann the Great, dazzled audiences with his stage routine, in which objects such as cards, coins, oranges, gloves, and rabbits appeared and disappeared in quick succession. Many of these effects relied on items hidden inside his jacket. One evening, Herrmann began his show and realized he was wearing the theater manager's jacket instead of his own. Instead of panicking, he told his assistant to find the manager and began doing fancy card flourishes. When the manager was found, Herrmann ducked off stage, swapped jackets, and then calmly began his original routine as if nothing had happened.

WHEN DISASTER STRIKES

If something goes wrong—for example, someone spots a hidden gimmick or you fumble a sleight—don't be downhearted. Make a joke or shrug it off, and move on quickly. If people are enjoying the show, they won't mind, and they'll forget about it once you've impressed them with your next trick.

Sometimes you can work a mistake into the act. Let's say you've dropped a palmed coin. Bend over to pick it up, making sure one foot is very near the coin.

Pretend to pick up the coin, but instead lift your toes slightly and slide the coin under your foot as you close your hand.

Pretend to move the coin to the other hand. One after the other, open your hands to show that the coin has disappeared!

TRICK OF THE TRADE

Keep spare coins in your pocket. If you're hiding a coin under your foot, take out another and do the Human Piggy-Bank vanish (page 13). Shake your body, then your leg, and then lift your foot to reveal that the coin has fallen right through you!

AND FINALLY . . .

Never end your act with a vanish. It's much more satisfying for your audience if you finish by producing something—either an object which vanished earlier or something unexpected. And always remember to return money or other valuables that volunteers have lent you!

Glossary

conjurer
another word for magician; Traditionally, conjurers make things appear and disappear.

escapologist
someone who performs escapology; This involves breaking free from constraints such as ropes, chains, handcuffs, cages, and crates. Many escapology tricks are dangerous, so don't try them yourself!

evaporate
to change from a solid or liquid into a gas

flourish
a fancy or showy move that makes a trick look more impressive

illusion
an effect that tricks you into thinking something impossible is happening

misdirection
the skill of drawing people's attention away from something you don't want them to see or think too much about

palming
hiding an object, such as a coin or a card, in the palm of your hand so it can't be seen

patter
prepared, practiced speech that magicians use when performing magic tricks; Although you need to work out your patter beforehand, make sure you speak naturally and don't read it out like a script.

prop
short for property; any object you use to help perform a trick

pull
a stretchy cord or band that is hidden under a magician's clothes and used to whip an object away up their sleeve as part of a vanishing trick

sleight-of-hand
the technique of secretly moving, altering, or swapping objects to create a magical effect; Sleights (pronounced "slights") take a lot of practice to perform well and rely on good misdirection skills.

slipknot
a knot that can be easily untied by pulling the free ends

street magic
magic tricks that are performed outside, often for small groups of people who gather around the magician to watch

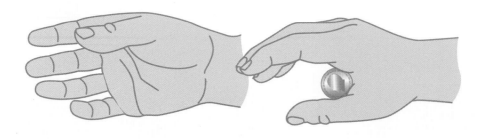

Web Sites

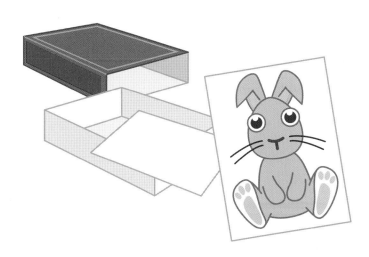

www.magictricks.com/library
Read biographies of famous magicians and discover fascinating facts about
their lives and the tricks they invented.

www.themagictricksblog.com/other-tricks/criss-angels-party-trick-using-a-toothpick/
Watch Criss Angel perform the great toothpick vanish from page 17.
You can also follow links to videos of more amazing tricks.

www.ehow.com/video_2374840_the-french-drop-illusion-magic.html
Learn how to do a perfect French Drop with this very useful guide.

www.activitytv.com/magic-tricks-for-kids
Find helpful video tutorials for all kinds of vanishing tricks, including many
from this book.

www.card-trick.com/unusual_card_tricks/the_vanishing_ace.htm
Learn how to make the ace of hearts disappear from a deck of cards as well as multiple
other card vanishing tricks.

www.magician.org/
Learn about the history of the International Brotherhood of Magicians, the world's
largest organization for those interested in or practicing magic. Find magic shows,
lectures, and conventions near you!

Index

SECRETS OF MAGIC . . . REVEALED!

Page 4: How did David Copperfield make the Statue of Liberty disappear?

Answer: *One theory is that the viewing platform where the audience sat was designed to rotate very smoothly and slowly. As a huge curtain was raised to cover the Statue of Liberty on Ellis Island, the platform may have moved (along with the curtain) so that the audience was actually facing the open sea. When the curtain was then dramatically lowered, it seemed as if the statue had gone. Whatever the case, the illusion must have taken a lot of ingenious machinery and painstaking planning. It was created by Jim Steinmeyer, a brilliant designer of mind-boggling special effects in theaters and theme parks.*

Page 8: How can the cupcake vanish before you walk back in the room?

Answer: *Go out, and then crawl back in on your hands and knees and grab the cupcake from the table. Eat it while sitting on the floor, and then crawl out again. Walk back in the room and, sure enough, the cupcake has disappeared.*

Page 10: How did Morritt's donkey and Houdini's elephant disappear?

Answer: *There was a large mirror placed diagonally inside the box. The animal was hidden behind this mirror, so when the audience thought they saw an empty box, they were in fact looking at half of the box, plus its reflection.*